blue.

A COLLECTION OF POETRY
ON HEALING, GRACE AND THE SEA

BAELEY HATHAWAY

Copyright © 2017 by Baeley Hathaway

Interior Design: Aaron Snethen

Cover Design and Graphics: Alyse Neal

All rights reserved. No part of this book may be reproduced in any form or by any electronic or mechanical means including information storage and retrieval systems without written permission from the publisher, except for a reviewer who may quote brief passages in a review.

Published in Boise, Idaho, by B.E.H. Poetry

ISBN: 9781945537066

E-Book ISBN: 9781945537073

Library of Congress Control Number: 2017952440

This book may be published in bulk for educational, business, organizational, or promotional use.

Printed in the United States of America. All rights reserved under international copyright law. Contents and/or cover may not be reproduced in whole or in part in any form without the express written consent of the publisher.

blue. is a collection of poetry on grace,
healing and the sea.

for every ocean that tries to drown us, for every storm that traps us under the waves, for all the black and blue, for all pain that surrounds us: we have an entire ocean inside, raging back. We can rise to the top. We can sing survival songs so loud, the shells sing them back to us forever. We don't have to be afraid of the sharks. We are brave. We are strong. We are alive, and there is no more beautiful a testament than this.

blue. is praising the sea as a rising force
of resilience.

all I could ever hope for these poems to become is a small collection of words that make you stop— if not for just a single moment— to feel hope in your heart that you will survive the storm, that you will discover the resilient, strong, and beautiful blue sea within you.

Baeley Hathaway

this is for you.

for your black and blue. for your strong heart. for your bravery.

this is for you.

I.
Love as a paperweight. holding us still and down and
beneath. I stay despite the wind.
peace as a straight jacket. holding blue between our fingertips and
letting it drip off our nail beds like rain
him, crooked smile,
him, broken heart,
he asks what would happen if
I woke up blind
what would you remember best? what would stay crystal clear?

II.
His eyes, I want to say, his eyes,
but I don't. I don't because I am alone.
I can hear my heartbeat against the sheets
like pressing my ear to a shell and breaking at
the cry of the ocean:
survival songs so fragile we can still hear them ringing.
I sing back to the wailing sea,
you're okay, you're okay.
She's drowning in the blue,
I understand. She's just alone.

◦ ◦ ◦

* * *

III.
I harbor fear in every empty space
the grey of it builds in the
whites of my eyes. It takes so much bravery
to look into them without flinching. He doesn't.
I know that no one
can stop a storm with just their hands even
if they're brave enough to stay in the eye of it.
It's just that, I am
memorizing
what's crystal clear

IV.
I find that peace
embraces you like linen wraps
the dead
Mummified with the gentle hands of priests
Amulets
to protect you from evil and
gold all around.

Both a sting
and a drop of honey
come from the same thing.

I understand.

Tell me about how
you've always been the boy
whose eyes hold entire oceans,
and I'll tell you about how
I've always been the girl
who can't stop singing about salt.

Just you and your body.
rise to the top.
rise from the middle of the sea.
rise and fill your lungs.
every breath means
you are alive, alive, alive
and there is no more beautiful a testament than this.

Even on the days it is too heavy to carry and
falls like sinking stones,

I want your submarine heart.

absolutely I will dive any depth for you,
absolutely I will stay beneath the waves,
come up for air for the both of us.

this is to say,
I'm not afraid of the sharks.
the first time I saw one,
I had to keep myself from touching it.

I said grace to the God who turns salt
to holy water and
took love by the gulp.

I want to go to the ocean with you.
I want to know what you taste like
after a day of salt
and wind
and my hands.

You're the city I want to come home to.
the stretch of land in the heart of the sea.

I'll never look at the world the same again.
not after you.

no matter where I go,
I'll know the sweetness of you,
how the ocean washes over me and
takes everything sour,
how salt water heals
even the worst of wounds.

seventy percent of the earth is sea,
and I could drown in just the depths of you.

I.
I wish I'd stayed when the bees came,
our own plague. I wish I'd iced the wounds with frozen peas,
kissed yours until the swelling stopped.
I wish I'd stayed through the pain,
said, "I'd rather cover myself in honey and
lay in the hive than let go of us."
but, I grew up where summers are hot and
sweet as nectar yet I still ran at the sound of the buzz.
I never learned how to calm the fear of the sting.
I learned to run.
I learned to run.

II.
I tried staying when the bees came,
covered myself in honey and called it a sacrifice,
held my breath through the stings.
I tried the frozen peas, but everything was so swollen
I could barely see straight.
no one recognized me through all the red,
all the burn, all the hurt. I didn't recognize myself.

I stayed despite this. but
compromise and love are not synonyms.
it took skin full of stingers to learn the difference.
that sometimes, love does mean leaving.
that sometimes, love does mean walking away.

I was brave to run
at the sound of the buzz.

I ran to a place sweet and full of nectar,
where love
means removing each reminder of you from my palms
until they heal.
I am healing.

Understand that
despite any black and blue,
love—
if it is good love—
will be more healing
than it is wound.

Love says, you do not have to do this alone.
Love says, if alone is what you are,
you can do this all the same.

In another world,
we were never supposed to choose someone else.
I don't have to keep saying,
"I love you but we both know
this isn't working,"
"I love you but that is not enough."

In another world, love is always enough
and our palms read each other's names,
no matter how many times we have them read.

the universe always says,
"you are exactly where you're supposed to be,
don't let go, don't let go."

and we never do. In this other world,
we hold on.

here, we let go because we have to.
because we keep pushing each other down
in order to stay up but
we love each other,
we do,

it just isn't enough.

No matter how fierce,
there are spaces even love cannot fill.

refreshing is
to soak in the cool blue of
your eyes and for a small,
beautiful second,
call drowning holy.

You say,
"what if in another universe, we never met?
what if we lived in the same city and passed each other on the
street and were nothing more than two strangers?"

"In another universe," I say,
"I'd recognize your lips even if every person in the world
stood on the same street."

I want to scream at the top of my lungs.
I want to bang on the belly of the beast and
demand he teach me
to be strong.
to survive the forest,
the trees
the darkness
all the fear that leaves me
undone.

I am so undone.

but I am learning to be the girl
who stops running away from herself.
I am learning to weave all the unraveled parts of me
back together into sailor's knots,
tie them so tight I'd have to throw
myself into the sea to undo them—

I refuse to ever drown again.

* * *

. . .

I am tired of staying in the blue.
I am building,
with my own two hands,
a place to anchor this heart.

I am learning to take my shadow back from the trees.
to confront my darkness and say,
come into the day.
see what can happen with just
a second of wild bravery.

There is an old, empty feeling inside my heart.
It's been there so long,
I call it friend.
I call it love.

The sadness of it all
swallows you up,
suddenly you are missing everyone that's ever touched you.
your skin gains a life of its own
shouts and pleads for someone to hold it.

aloneness is so heavy,
it piles on top your chest so strong,
you don't move for days.
you lay still. you try to breathe.
you curse at the people who've left.
curse at yourself for chasing them or
for letting them go.

darkness accumulates like storm clouds.
it starts pouring, you shiver and shake,
you stare in horror as your house
floods with the grief.

that is the way of pain.
it demands you let it wreck you,
so when the foundation falls and rots,
you find yourself having to start over.

● ● ●

. . .

it is the way of pain
to force you to grow.

sometimes it's still too painful
to think of growth this way.
that is all okay.
you lay still.
you try to breathe.

When sadness is a cocoon
wrapped around your body too tight,
your heart will swell and
your bones will crack
and the whole world will turn cold.
everything becomes painful like your skin
is full of thorns with no sign
of anything blooming.
your lungs will turn to stone as
your collarbones cave in, shattering inside
you like a sheet of glass.

even if
you fall to the ground,
eventually, you will find strength.
It will emerge from your broken parts,
more raging ocean
than leaking wounds.
you will use it to break out from the shell you've become.

some people are born knowing how to swim and others
have to nearly drown first.
you will always know what that means.

you are stronger for it.
you are blooming.

hope resides in very small spaces.
you have to look very, very hard and
squint your eyes to the sun, slowing down
your steps to search
between sidewalk cracks and
smile lines and
old jean pockets.

you will learn, ever so slowly,
that hope, everywhere you look,
crystallizes right there before your eyes.

this is the magic
of how deeply you are loved.
the earth is always ready to sprinkle it wherever you go.
it is always
ready when you are.

you can give your whole heart
to everyone in the world,
but first, give it to yourself.
you deserve this much.

I won't apologize for the way I love.
it's whole.
it's all. it's every drop I have, every time.
I've never known how to keep my heart safe,
I've only ever learned how to rebuild from brokenness,
make a castle from ruin,
willingly opening my heart so wide,
entire storms make it in to tear it apart.

I'm sorry if it is too strong for you,
but I will always live my life this way.
open hearted.
transparently so.

I want to be a woman so rooted in the earth
that its light and love
flow into me no matter
what turns my heart inside out.

I.
You saved my life once.
you didn't even know it.
It was that Friday night this time last year,
when I called late at night just to ask for a prayer, and
you called back just to say one.
the whole world was weeping that night.
hours and hours on end, it didn't stop.
the sky knew I needed to rest.
It poured so I didn't have to.

I feel like the place people go to leave all
the parts of them that need fixing.
my hands are always holding together
everything but my own heart.

you are the place I go to rest.
the place that feels more like home than any four walls could.
you are the quiet. the calm. the refuge
I take to remember
this is who I am. this is what
I believe. look at my strong heart.
look at all I've built with my own two hands.

something about your heart and my heart and mending.

II.
Earthquakes always split the earth in all the wrong places,
down the spine of countries.
through the heart of big cities.
maybe the curve of Spain used to fit within the Oregon coast,
and for years and years they've been mourning for
the way it felt to fit into another body—
to not have to keep pulling the sea so close,
letting salt heal the wound
missing leaves.

even when two things are tightly bound together,
the earth will separate them if she needs to.
this is the best I know to say,
if your spine is the coast of Oregon, and
my hips are the curve of Spain,
I'd spend years and years missing how
it feels being close to you.
I think I always would.

I'd pull the sea close, kiss its shore,
whisper *I miss you, I miss you,* into every shell that washes up
and hope it finds it's way to you.

* * *

. . .

If we could lay beneath a map of the world and
imagine all the different ways this could have gone,
all the places we could have ended up,
I'd always tell you,

even if we had been born across the world from each other,
we'd end up somewhere in the middle at the same time,
I know it, I know it, and it would feel like the place
I go to rest, to remember, this is who I am, this is what I believe.
look at my strong heart.
look at all I've made with my own two hands.
look at how beautifully life falls together.
my ribcage is a makeshift storm shelter and
you can take refuge here.

I want to hold everything sweet/
everything holy/ between my teeth/
savor the way/
honey tastes on the tongue/

I know/ that an entire lifetime/
is so much more/ than the sweet/
and the holy/ and/
bright things fall apart/
like stars in space/ even when
you think they'll burn forever/
but love/ even so/ everyday is
a small lifetime/
and I will gladly take your arms as
a deathbed/

I just want to love you loudly.
so loud the whole world can hear.

harsh seasons will come/
and you will feel like/
all your bones turned to stone/
like everything is so heavy you can't/
get out from under all/
the hurt/ all the trying to run away/ but finding/
the pain
is inside you/
and has grown like yellow weeds/
in a garden/
that was never supposed/
to grow/
in the first place.
they are beautiful/
but they're taking up all the space/
for good things/
they are beautiful/
but they've stolen the sunlight/
from everything else/

You'll find hope in places you never thought it'd be/
in your best friend's eyes as they fall asleep/
in the lavender you buy for the kitchen table/
in the nights you don't sleep because everything hurts/
in Sunday mornings/
in grief/

you'll find grief comes in dull waves/
like blades of grass/
you'll find it between pages/
in crystallized honey/ when sweet things change/
grief in the upside down bouquets
of dried lilies pinned to your wall/
when alive things die/
when you can't let them go/

If I had to imagine God, he's blue silk bed sheets, and
all day he sings in low octaves:
Welcome. Bienvenidos. Karibu. Willkommen. Velkomin. Maeva.
all grief, all hope, all the mess in between.
Welcome.

I cannot
carry the weightlessness of my existence in my hands
without weeping, anymore.
anymore, I am harboring fragility like the small, blue
robin's egg I found in my grandmother's yard when
I was small and I held it in my hands so gentle I
thought any second, life would emerge.
but it began to crack
and the heart leaked death so strong
I thought the whole town would smell it and
grieve as intensely as I.

even the things we think we can save, we end up losing.

It's not our fault. It's our condition to hold on.
temporary is coded into our DNA and into the veins.
maybe we bleed red to remind us soon,
it will stop.
all of it.
like a traffic light. like a siren. our lungs
and the hurt and the love, too, and
this is the tragedy of endings.

sometimes
the things we love
are the most temporary of all.

when the world felt backwards,
you became point north.
the place I'd look to find home.

when I look at the sky, I think of this.
how the constellations stay the same even
when the people don't.

how stars are much less risky than
the human heart.

you are a backwards road map.
leading me in circles that still
feel like home.

I'd always hoped you'd open up just enough
for the light to seep in.
just enough for the honey.
after that first taste, how it stays in the throat,
you'd think of my lips
and suddenly, you'd taste it—
how sweet love can be.

but love
is not supposed
to feel like getting stung.
every time we touch
it feels like putting my hands into a hive and
expecting softness.

I'm not claiming to be the honey.
I'm more bee than anything else.

I just don't know what to do with the things I love
if not to hold on and hold on tighter,

even
if I should be more snake
than bee.

Isolation chains you to every fear
you've ever buried
as to not be crushed by it.

It's never the refuge you think it'll be.
you always end up
halfway in the middle, somewhere between
becoming part of the fear and
running away from it.

either way you're not really getting anywhere.

I wish I knew how to find a balance in this.
how to let go and move forward
all at the same time.

I know it takes so much boldness to be alive.
to be fearless. to find bravery.
to break enough chains, you emerge.
so here I am, digging.
for all of us.
for the hope of finding refuge
in one another, instead.

healing smells like
the earth after a long rain;
feels like watching the sun break through after
so much grey.

If I had to name it—
this embodiment of hope—
I'd call it grace.
the way it pours freely.

I've learned that nothing feels as safe
as the gentle boldness of hearts
unreserved in their love,
unafraid of the mess of mending, and

If, a human life were measured in grit,
they'd sit through the storm
with gladness running through their veins
like lightning strikes:
these people of grace.
these people that hold
bold and gentle love between fingertips—
healing
like the salt of the earth.

ask me to talk you off the ledge
of leaving this world and
darling I will find you,
I will find you at the top of any mountaintop, and say,
this is as close to the stars as we will get, see,
because soon enough,
we will dance on them and soon enough,
we will call the moon home
but for now, darling,
we are here with beating hearts.

we can talk about how this world feels more dark
than light, sometimes, and how
tenderness is a forgotten art, and how
easy it is to feel achingly, innately alone,
but how

we are not.

we can cultivate light and practice tenderness,
stay together so close we become
two bodies,

one heart, two bodies, one soul, two bodies,

one beautiful mess of love and brokenness.

tell me you don't want me to go after all.

tell me you know a star is just a star but
you'll follow it North until you find me, anyways.

———————

All I really have left to do is
take all my love to the backyard and
bury all I have for you.

which is so, so much.
which will take all of the strength I have.

I am a reservoir
of all I have lost.
every past version of myself
I have laid to rest,
buried in the rose garden,
picked from the ground and hung upside down
I watch them dry up
I watch them crumble
I keep them pinned to the wall for far too long
or maybe just long enough
until they fall petal by petal,
backwards into the flowerbed of all
my almosts.

I lay at the shore of all that has made me,
feel life run over my skin.
I have lost. I have held on.
I have always become better.

I am enough. I am enough.
all of me, all of the time.

I am whole and strong and worthy.
all of me. all of the time,
I am enough.

You can be honest as well as strong.
you can embrace vulnerability
as well as stand on your own.
you do not have to choose
between being respected and
being soft.

never mistake being misunderstood for being defective.
you are who you are
and that alone
is enough.

this is how you use tenderness to heal wounds:
hold broken together so delicately,
it mends.

---

burying all my love into the earth is like
swallowing an entire ocean and calling it a sip.
like pretending I can harbor it
without also drowning.

but I will learn.
I will throw myself at the earth
until it has been returned to the flowerbeds,
turned to water that flows through the veins and
fills what was empty.

until I can watch flowers grow without
thinking of your hands.

maybe we've done this all before/ in some other lifetime/
this dance of hearts/ this rooted love/
that by the time we got here/
to this time/
this place/
we'd already merged souls so close/ there
wasn't any space left/ between them/

so maybe that's why I feel so whole/
when you're around/
like finding home/
like waking up to a world that finally makes sense/
because in this time/
in this place/
we are here/
and the earth/ she let us meet again/
and again and again/ and again/
our dancing hearts/ our rooted love/
in this lifetime/ in the next.

Isn't it stunning how this life works?

the harsh season
folded my body like
origami hearts,
paper cranes
so thin, broken called
me by name.

because of this I have
become more woman than girl.
more brave than afraid.
more wild than anything tame.

It is within the ruin
I have learned grit.

where I can say from the eye of the storm,

hope has been my middle name.
hope has surrounded me.

my hands have made all wreckage
a home.
it always keeps its doors open.

* * *

• • •

as softness came,
I took my body,
my fragile heart,
and folded it into a love note.

It sings of the bravery.
of the resilience.
of the hope that has defined me. a love note
to all I have been, am, and will be.

there is a river. God flows there.
I could pass my life watching it move,
watching the green come and the animals drink and
the sky pouring it's tears into the banks.
there is a river and God washes his hands there.
I can tell because it ripples.
I can tell because when I soak in it,
everything heals. even my insides.

My name is crescent moon.
My name is forest green.
My name is creature fear and I call myself brave.

I pour myself like split open fruit,
spill all my red blood into the river.
I cry because it stays clear.
I cry because there is a place in this world
that doesn't stain with my hurt,
but washes it away.

* * *

. . .

behind the city lights, underneath our moon.
we are named by the stars.
we are called spring.
we are called children.

we cut each other by the chests
just to make sure we still have beating hearts and
some of us do and
some of us don't but
at the river, where God flows, we are washed clean.
made blue.

Rivers are always moving towards the same sea.
here is my promise: your love is safe with me.
I am holding it close, and mine flows free.

I have this dream where we come together like
how rivers flow into one ocean,
how the sea is stronger and deeper because of it.

the poem I never want to write is the one where I say,
my love is a river flowing North, and yours, South,
but instead of meeting in the middle,
they run parallel, never crossing.

the poem I never want to write is the one where I say,
sometimes, you have to let go,
even if it makes your chest feel full of bees.

my chest is full of bees.

each time I think of this,
I think of the sea—
how mesmerizing a body I could drown in.

Heartache is what leads you home.

through the forest,
through miles and miles of open road,
all I know to cry is

I am on my way.
I am on my way.

The scars will always be there.
and sometimes, will hurt
like open wounds, but they are
proof of your body's ability to make you
whole again.
you will be whole again.

at the very heart of me,
in the blood that flows, in the bones that ache,
Is a thirst to be so close to another living thing that we
cannot tell where one body ends
and the other begins.

with the thirst, in the veins, in the marrow,
is the gnawing desire to be always alone.
to be so entwined with solitude it
fits the curve of my body
like a lover.

I hold everything that aches. I have always known
how to mend
all on my own.

I mourn endings
with all the passion I carry.
grief of things lost
lingers hot in my blood.
mending all on my own has always been a balancing act,
like at any moment, my fingertips could slip
and then what would I do
with all this tenderness?
what would I do
with all these poems?

it's never been easy to let go.
but what I learn with each goodbye is
to become a home.

one that sometimes crumbles.
one that always rebuilds.

one that knows, all the time, sure as the night,
it is okay to be alone.
it is okay and it is beautiful to be alone.

my grandmother
has always kept a journal of the birds that go for winter
and return for spring.
in her neat, loopy cursive, she notes the severity of winter,
the quality of nests,
the pattern of coming and going.

no matter how harsh a season,
she has fifty years of proof
that the sun has always come back.
the frozen lake thaws. the birds return.

I hold close her faith in the natural way of things.
her steadfastness that each going is for the best,
each coming is more beautiful than the last,
and that no matter how cold,
how unbearable changing seasons can be,
of course spring is on her way.
bringing life and
survival and
new beginnings.

may your tears only fall into your deepest hurt,
the kind that feel like black holes,
that pull your world off its axis,
that bring you to your knees.

may your tears fall there like rainwater,
until flowers have grown into thick forests
in all your empty spaces.

until every hurt sings of regrowth.

when it comes to the letting go of
things that have wrapped itself around you like ivy,
it is easy to forget that despite
the loss, you are still whole.

you hold on so long and so tight,
you learn how to live comfortably with your hands
full of poison.

just because you know how, doesn't mean it's healthy.

one day you will be able to look back and
be indescribably thankful that you allowed
yourself to keep moving forward.
you granted yourself the freedom
to make space
for something new.

despite everything.
you are still whole.
you are overflowing.

here is my love, here is my love,
always, always.

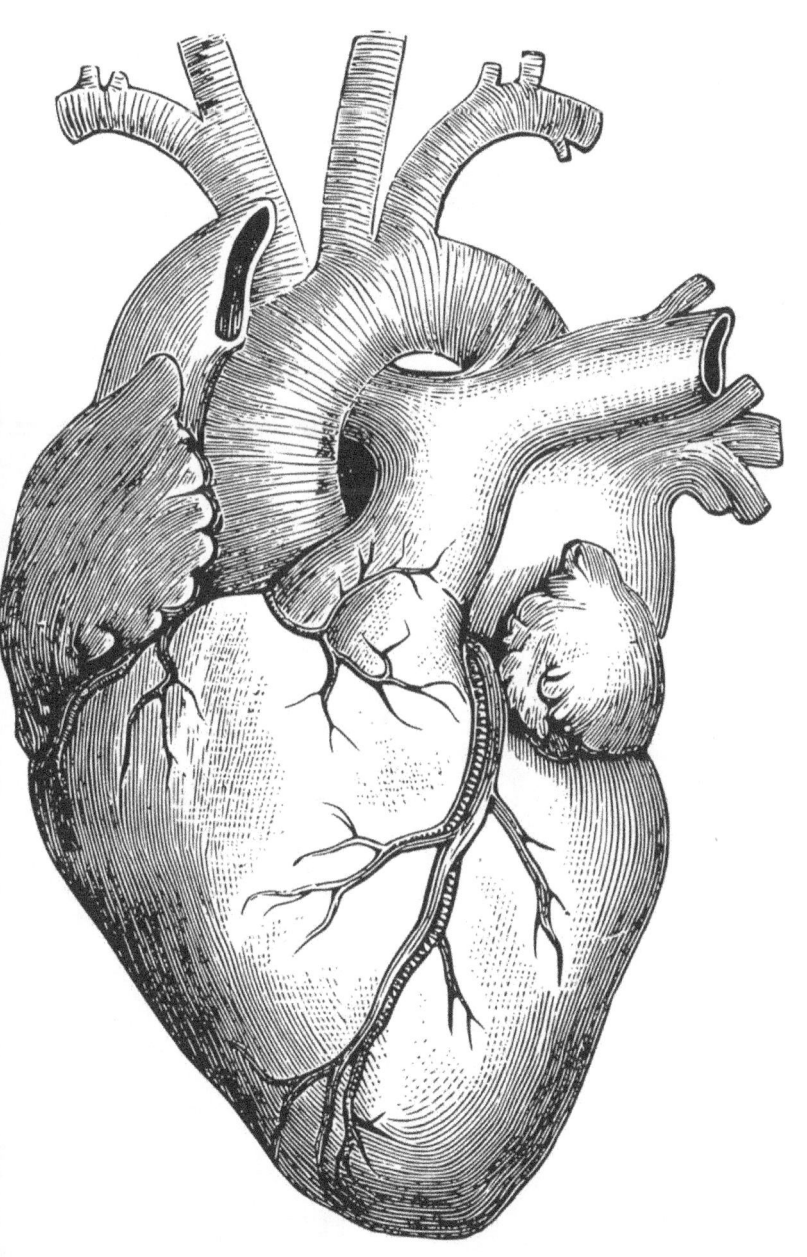

all I know
is that if anything is going to break my heart,
I want it to be you.

I worry for my fragile heart.
I worry about the rain and the lightning and
how these nights are full of them.
by that I mean, my whole world is a storm,
and I am howling like the wind.

I am mourning.
I am mourning.

all my heart ever does when I ask it to be brave
is skip a beat.

I forgive her despite this.
I love her unveiled softness.
the world needs more of that.

dear fragile heart/
I am so sorry/
for always leaving you behind/
for ignoring all the ways in which you break/ because it hurts/
it hurts/
I am so sorry/
for being a careless home/
I have broken/
all my ribs and/
left you vulnerable and open and/
I didn't even tell you when I'd return/ I didn't say/ good luck/
goodbye/ thank you/
it's just sometimes/
when the world is heavy/
I wish you were a bit stronger/
I get angry at the blood that is/
always all over the place/ I get angry/
that you can't hold it/
together/
when I need you to/ oh/

· · ·

• • •

my fragile heart/
you who are always dripping honey/
bleeding it all over everything you love/
don't listen/ to my anger/
keep breaking/ keep loving/ keep bleeding/
the world needs more of/
something so sweet/

each quiet moment, each soft touch,
I keep safe,
guard in my pockets,
twirl in my fingers and
think of your hands.

how they unlock me.

poets
love to write about peaches and
now I understand why.
you love something until you're pitted.
until all sweet does
is make your stomach ache.

I could turn all this love to ash and
it would still be love,
it just wouldn't look the same.

this is all to say that
sometimes, loving well
means the same thing as
walking away.

To be a person of love, to be a person
who forgives and gives,
you have to hold on only to the people and places
that overflow in you what was already full.

you have to know that you have never had
something missing. you were whole
before you ever had to let go and you will still
be whole afterwards.

sometimes the best thing you can do
is leave
in search of a place
that doesn't take so much of you.

It's like how on airplanes,
you have to put the mask on yourself before anyone else.
it's protocol, your own survival.
so don't take it lightly.

breathe for yourself first, always.

the season of mending.
of surrender.
of breaking bones so they heal up right.
assessing the damage and beginning again.

the season of enough.
knowing I am enough for myself.
letting go of those who make me question it.

the season of grit.
lavender and planting seeds to see them grow.
new recipes, curled hair, bold outfits.

the season of new. looking up.
really seeing.
of love. sweet as syrup.

this is how the whole world will come to an end:
no fire, no storm;
but you and I separated by trees and
wind and
miles of open road.

I miss you, I miss you, I miss you.

the kind of missing that stops hearts.

"what if all love turns sour?
what if it ferments like fruit and
after a while we forget how sugar tastes?"

"then we'll do what people have always done,
we'll make something new.
we'll turn sour love into sweet wine and
drink from the cup every morning.
by night, we'll be so drunk, we'll kiss like teenagers,
like no time has ever passed."

When I think of home, I think of you.

letting go of hurt doesn't work the way holding on to it does.
hurt becomes a stubborn part of you.
hurt becomes your best friend, because it has stuck around when everything else has left.
hurt becomes you.
and you've heard all about the letting go.
you've been trying to do so for so, so long.

the truth of the matter is, romanticizing your pain
has made leaving it behind a battle you haven't won.
all you can do well is hold on.

there is no metaphysical garden
you can go to bury the love you have
for people who couldn't love you back.
no matter how desperately you dig.
no matter how deep the roots have grown.

there is no flood that will come
to wash away all the parts of you that are more spice than sugar,
more sharp edges than anything soft.
I know you want to drown the hurt.
I know you want to cleanse the heart.

• • •

. . .

no fire will come burning down the walls
you've built around yourself,
a brick added each time you thought you'd healed
just to find that with each new beginning,
the wounds are open wide.
the wounds burn and burn and burn.

as much as you wish it were this easy.
there is no garden. no flood. no fire.
there is only the constant choice to be
healing and growing and moving on.

this is where the fight begins—
you have to dig yourself out of this one small victory at a time.
it is not easy, but it is worth it.
healing is worth all your grit.

even if love gets left to the earth,
it goes and grows itself a garden.
there's no matter of digging to uproot it.

this has become my anthem, the new beat of my heart.

I want to drown the hurt,
I want to cleanse the heart.

It's the rain that will come and wash away
all the parts of me that are more spice than sugar,
more sharp edges than anything soft.
It's time to retire my aching hands.
stop digging up so much dirt.

I will live in a garden full of love, even the kind with thorns,
if only the earth promises
to always water what grows.
open heart, empty hands, pouring everything she has,

she does.

she does.

you tell them they are worthy of love.
you always let them know you are proud of them.
you hold their hand in the car.
you read the books they read, just to understand their mind.
you write them love letters, send them in the mail.
you notice when their day has been too long and
hold them until a new one begins.
you let them cry into your chest,
laugh at your jokes, and you always, always say,
I love you. I love you. I am your safe place.

This is how you love them.

if you pour yourself too much into another person,
the heart will learn how to bleed sideways.
after a while, it wouldn't know what to do
without it's second heart.
it wouldn't know what to do with
all that blood.

I heard a theory once
that the world is full of invisible strings
connecting us heart to heart to those who enter
and leave our lives.

It said our fingertips
are a roadmap of everyone we've touched,
our hearts the place strings are tied in bows.
the world is made of love crossing and tangling,
bridging gaps thousands of miles wide.

when I feel alone,
I look at my hands and imagine
whose heart they're connected to.

I pull them through the air and hope
that the tug at the heart will remind them of
warmth and of home,
even through the distance
even through the time and all the
growing that comes with it.

* * *

how can I love well enough to sew damaged hearts
back together?

how can I weave art from chaos,
make something beautiful while
I am alive
and full of love?

I have always been all or nothing.

there have been so many days
I fall into the nothingness
as if empty space could be a home.

now my bones burn blue.

I want to be everything.

when I think of the stars,
I think of you and
your gentle bravery,
me and my wild heart.

you have taken all wilderness,
all wind and storm,
all roaming of my soul,
and made a home.

a star has never been just a star.
not after you.
not after you followed them north until you found me,
until we made our way
in love and light.

I can hardly believe
the audacity
of my own heart
to wreck itself
the way it has.

anxiety tangles my stomach into knots
like pirates taking down a ship.
I may just be lying here, but I feel like I'm sinking.

I want to jump ship from this body,
dive into a sea
that drowns all this ache.

my chest is a dam almost breaking.
even when I am tying to let go, let go—
I overflow.

I am a paradox
of together and apart.
afraid and fearless. trusting and tight fisted.
I can't be anything but.

I put my hand to my chest
gentle like a sheet of snow
and say:

please, aching heart, slow down.
you are okay. you are safe.
every knot works itself free.

let peace wash over you like waves.
hear the fear leave your body,
pass your ears on its way out,
so all that's left to listen to is your cadence.
a lullaby.
you have always been the perfect love song.

goodnight, goodnight, my aching heart.
joy comes in the morning.

my heart is a compass
that always leads back to love.

---

maybe this is the bravest thing of all:
to know love can drain all your blood and break all your bones,
but to open your chest, expose your heart,
and offer all you are anyways.

to bleed and break and bruise,
and choose love every time.
choose love every time.

we romanticize the stars and hope
they lead us home.
but sometimes all they do is burn.
they collapse into themselves,
implode into scattered light before we
ever make it out.
all the grit in the world can't
fill that empty space.

I gaze up at the sky anyway,
notice the stars all point to the same thing:
I praise the moon in all her quiet bravery.
she carries all the grief of the world,
spilling it into storm clouds, river streams, ocean waves,
our hearts and our veins.

this is why when we rest,
there is a heaviness we feel to our bones—

we carry hurt this way
so others don't have to.

I stand here
in all my aliveness, and
keep believing in the goodness of the world.
even in all the quiet defeat.
even in all the grief.

the year of humility and surrender/
of putting myself first/ a love all-consuming/
the year of soft/ pastel colored skies/
of honey/ so much honey/
the year I stopped calling lost loves during bouts of loneliness/
the year of intense/
swirling loneliness/ of navigating it alone/
the year of learning to be gentle with my own skin/
tender with my own heart/
the year of understanding/
of missing/
tearing down and/
building again/
the year of apologizing to my fragile heart/of hurting it anyways/
of promises/
nightmares/sleepless nights/ tangible fear/
the year of darkness/
and light/
the fight between the two/
growing pains/sunshine and/
pouring rain/ of new beginnings/
of letting go/
of digging myself out of depression/
with my bare hands/

hallelujah to the middle of June. to the gods who made us.

hallelujah to our broken love song. our hymn of almost.
to the space between us.
to the golden moon for loving the other side of the world
even though she can't get there. for bleeding across the whole sky
trying to reach it anyway.

hallelujah, hallelujah
to my wholeness. to your missing parts.
to my empty hands. to your guarded heart.

sometimes stars don't become brighter when they collide,
they just burst.
and all the ash is still love.
it just doesn't look the same.

● ● ●

* * *

hallelujah to our burned hands.
to burying it all like a shrine of what could have been.
to growing grief alongside us
like flowers on a gravestone.

hallelujah to our preservation.
our close call.
the end of a drought.
to the other side of the world, the stars it holds,
the light still rising from the East.

hallelujah, hallelujah
to the middle of June. to the middle of June.

ABOUT BAELEY HATHAWAY

Baeley Hathaway is a poet from Coeur d' Alene, Idaho. You can most likely find her writing in a coffee shop, reading at the lake, hanging out with family, or embarking on a trip to a new country.

Baeley has never been afraid to share the interworking of her heart and mind. She found that outlet in poetry, often leaving them around the house, on the Internet, or for others to find. blue. is the first collection of these poems, and if nothing else, a window for others to not feel alone.

www.ingramcontent.com/pod-product-compliance
Lightning Source LLC
Chambersburg PA
CBHW061333040426
42444CB00011B/2905